the joy of entertaining

by Taryn Scarfone
JOY FILLED EATS

table of contents

Chapter One

hot appetizers

oven baked parmesan garlic wings

 5 MINS

 30 MINS

 35 HR

These Oven Baked Parmesan Garlic Wings are the perfect snack or dinner for football season. They are crispy, rich, and zesty with garlic, parmesan, and red pepper.

ingredients

- 5-6 lbs. whole chicken wings cut into sections
- 1 stick of butter melted
- 1/2 tsp Italian seasoning
- 1/2 cup Parmesan cheese
- 1 tsp garlic powder
- 1/16 tsp crushed red pepper
- 1/4 tsp salt
- 1 egg
- 1 stick of butter softened

directions

Preheat the oven to 425. Cut the wings into sections.

Put the wings on a rimmed baking sheet with a metal cooling rack on top. Make sure your cooling rack is oven safe before you try this. Cook for 15 minutes.

Make the sauce. Blend the butter, cheese, and seasonings in a small blender until combined. Add the egg and process until combined. The sauce is about the thickness of ketchup.

After 15 minutes remove the wings and flip them over. At this point, they are almost fully cooked. Turn on the broiler. Put the wings under the broiler for 5 min. Keep an eye on them so they don't burn. Remove them and flip again. Keep flipping and broiling until they are the desired crispness. They should definitely be 165 degrees by now but I always recommend checking with a meat thermometer.

Toss immediately in the sauce. The wings are hot enough that you shouldn't need to worry about using a raw egg in the sauce. It's similar to spaghetti carbonara in which you crack a raw egg over hot spaghetti. Garnish with extra cheese.

nutrition facts

Amount Per Serving: 1

Servings: 12 servings

Calories 116

Calories from Fat 72

Total Fat 8g (12%)

Saturated Fat 2g (10%)

Cholesterol 44mg (15%)

Sodium 87mg (4%)

Potassium 80mg (2%)

Total Carbohydrates 0g (0%)

Sugars 0g

Dietary Fiber 0g (0%)

Protein 9g (18%)

Vitamin A (1.9%)

Calcium (2.8%)

Iron (2.8%)

spinach & feta pastries

20 MINS

30 MINS

50 MINS

These handheld savory Spinach & Feta Pastries are my favorite vegetarian lunch, snack, or dinner. You don't even miss the meat when you bite into one. They are filling and delicious. You can eat them on their own or pair with soup or salad.

ingredients

DOUGH INGREDIENTS:

- 8 oz mozzarella cheese
- 2 oz cream cheese
- 1 cup almond flour
- 1/2 cup coconut flour
- 1 egg
- 1 tsp baking powder
- 1/2 tsp salt

FILLING INGREDIENTS

- 12 oz frozen spinach thawed and drained
- 4 oz crumbled feta cheese
- 1 egg white
- 1 tsp minced onion
- 1/2 tsp garlic powder
- pinch of salt
- 1 egg yolk to brush on the outside of the pastries

directions

Preheat the oven to 375.

Put the mozzarella and cream cheese in a microwave-safe bowl. Microwave one minute. Stir. Microwave 30 seconds. Stir. At this point, all the cheese should be melted. Microwave 30 more seconds until uniform and gloopy (it should look like cheese fondue at this point). Add the rest of the dough ingredients and the cheese to a food processor. Mix using the dough blade until a uniform color. If you do not have a food processor you can mix in a medium bowl with a wooden spoon but you may need to dump it onto wax paper and knead it by hand to thoroughly incorporate the ingredients.

Stir together the ingredients for the filling. Set aside the egg yolk to brush on the pastries.

Roll the dough out between two pieces of parchment paper into a 6 x 18 inch rectangle. Cut in half lengthwise with a pizza cutter. Put the filling down the center of one piece. Top with the other piece of dough. Use the pizza cutter to cut into 7 or 8 pieces. Put them on a baking sheet lined with parchment.

Gently press the edges together on two opposing sides of each pastry. Use a kitchen shears or small knife to make a few slits in the top dough. Brush with the egg yolk. Bake for 30 minutes until golden brown.

nutrition facts

Amount Per Serving: 1

Servings: 8

Calories 290

Calories from Fat 189

Total Fat 21g (32%)

Saturated Fat 9g (45%)

Cholesterol 87mg (29%)

Sodium 567mg (24%)

Potassium 274mg (8%)

Total Carbohydrate 11g (4%)

Dietary Fiber 5g (20%)

Protein 15g (30%)

Vitamin A (107.9%)

Calcium (3.4%)

Iron (11%)

stuffed mushrooms with cream cheese & ham

 10 MINS

 30 MINS

 40 MINS

If you are looking for an easy, impressive, 5 ingredient appetizer or side dish you've come to the right place! These Ham & Cheese Stuffed Mushrooms have about a 5 minute prep time but are SO much better than your standard restaurant appetizer mushrooms.

ingredients

- 8 large white mushrooms
- 3 oz cream cheese softened
- 1 1/2 cups shredded cheese (I used a two cheese blend of cheddar and monterey jack)
- 1 1/2 cups chopped deli ham
- 1 tsp garlic salt

directions

Preheat oven to 400.

Remove stems from mushrooms and discard or save for another use. Stir together all the other ingredients. Divide between the mushrooms.

Bake for 30 minutes or until mushrooms are softened and the filling is golden.

nutrition facts

Amount Per Serving: 1

Servings: 8 cupcakes

Calories 175

Calories from Fat 108

Total Fat 12g (18%)

Saturated Fat 6g (30%)

Cholesterol 44mg (15%)

Sodium 770mg (32%)

Potassium 286mg (8%)

Total Carbohydrate 2g (1%)

Dietary Fiber 0g (0%)

Protein 12g (24%)

Vitamin A (5.7%)

Vitamin C (1.4%)

Calcium (12%)

Iron (3.6%)

bacon jalapeno poppers

10 MINS

35 MINS

45 MINS

Bacon jalapeno poppers are the perfect appetizer or snack. Creamy and melted cheese inside of a spicy jalapeno pepper wrapped in a piece of delicious bacon with the perfect amount of ranch seasoning.

ingredients

- 4 jalapenos halved and seeded
- 4 oz cream cheese
- 1/4 cup cheddar cheese
- 1 tsp ranch seasoning
- 8 slices bacon (about 1/2 pound)

RANCH SEASONING:

- 1 tsp garlic powder
- 1 tsp onion powder
- 1 tsp parsley
- 1 tsp dill weed
- 1/2 tsp salt

directions

Preheat oven to 400.

Combine the cream cheese, cheddar cheese, and ranch seasoning. Mix well. Divide between the prepared jalapenos. Wrap each jalapeno half in a strip of bacon. Place on a metal rimmed baking sheet sprayed with nonstick cooking spray.

Bake for 35 minutes.

recipe notes

Ranch Seasoning:

If you'd like to make just enough ranch seasoning for this recipe use 1/4 of each spice listed and 1/8 tsp salt.

However, this blend is also great for dips and dressings. You can mix it into a combination of mayo, sour cream, and/or yogurt for an easy dip. Thin with unsweetened almond milk for dressing. You will need approximately 1.5 tbsp per cup but please season to taste.

nutrition facts

Servings: 12 cupcakes

Calories 96

Calories from Fat 72

Total Fat 8g (12%)

Saturated Fat 3g (15%)

Cholesterol 57mg (19%)

Sodium 67mg (3%)

Potassium 127mg (4%)

Total Carbohydrate 3g (1%)

Dietary Fiber 1g (4%)

Protein 3g (6%)

Vitamin A (36.9%)

Vitamin C (0.5%)

Calcium (4.6%)

Iron (4.7%)

french onion tartlets

15 MINS

1 HR 30 MIN

1 HR 45 MIN

If you like French onion soup you will love my French Onion Tartlets. With caramelized onions, toasted cheese, and a golden dough shell they are the perfect appetizer for entertaining.

ingredients

FILLING INGREDIENTS:

- 1 tbsp butter
- 1 tbsp olive oil
- 6 medium onions thinly sliced (about 4 cups)
- 1/2 tsp salt
- 7 oz garlic flavored cream cheese
- 4 slices Havarti Cheese

CRUST INGREDIENTS:

- 8 oz. mozzarella shredded or cubed
- 2 oz. cream cheese
- 1 egg
- 2/3 cup almond flour
- 4 tsp coconut flour
- 1 tsp baking powder
- 1/2 tsp salt

directions

Heat a large frying pan over medium-low heat. Add the olive oil and butter. Add the onions. Cook over medium-low, stirring occasionally until they are caramelized. To get them really nice and truly caramelized it takes about an hour. Low and slow is the way to go with onions. This is mostly hands-off time, just make sure to stir them every 10 minutes.

You can caramelize the onions the day before making the tarts. Just pop them in the refrigerator.

Meanwhile, preheat the oven to 350. Put the mozzarella and cream cheese in a microwave-safe bowl. Microwave one minute. Stir. Microwave 30 seconds. Stir. At this point all the cheese should be melted. Microwave 30 more seconds until uniform (it should look like cheese fondue at this point). Add the rest of the dough ingredients and the cheese to a food processor. Mix using the dough blade until a uniform color. If you do not have a food processor you can mix in a medium bowl with a wooden spoon but you may need to dump it onto wax paper and knead it by hand to thoroughly incorporate the ingredients.

Grease a 24 hole mini muffin tin. Divide the dough between the holes of the tin. Using wet fingers press it down into the bottom and up the sides of each hole. If your fingers aren't wet it will stick to your fingers. I keep a small bowl of water next to me while I work. I dip my hands, press two out, dip again, and repeat.

Once the onions are a golden brown turn off the heat and stir in the garlic flavored cream cheese.

Bake the tart shells for 6 minutes. Remove from the oven and divide the onion mixture between them. Top each with 1/6 of a slice of Havarti. Bake for 25 minutes until the cheese is bubbly and the crust is golden.

nutrition facts

Amount Per Serving: 1

Servings: 24

Calories 124

Calories from Fat 81

Total Fat 9g (14%)

Saturated Fat 4g (20%)

Cholesterol 31mg (10%)

Sodium 235mg (10%)

Potassium 87mg (2%)

Total Carbohydrate 4g (1%)

Dietary Fiber 1g (4%)

Sugars 1g

Protein 5g (10%)

Vitamin A (5.4%)

Vitamin C (2.4%)

Calcium (10.9%)

Iron (1.8%)

fried pickles

 10 MINS

 7 MIN

 17 MIN

Skip the oil and the mess and whip up these fried pickles that are baked in your oven or air fried in your air fryer! As good as a restaurant and healthier!

ingredients

FILLING INGREDIENTS:

- 12 pickle spears
- 1 cup coconut flour
- 2.5 ounce package pork rinds
- 2 large eggs

SAUCE INGREDIENTS:

- 8 ounces sour cream
- 1/2 tablespoon dried dill
- 1 teaspoon vinegar
- 1 teaspoons garlic powder
- 1/4 teaspoon pepper
- 1/2 teaspoon salt

directions

Slice spears in half the long way, and dry slightly with tea cloth or paper towel.

In a small bowl, beat eggs.

In a separate bowl add coconut flour.

Using a food processor or your hands, process/smash pork rinds until fine crumbs.

Add pork rind crumbs to a third bowl.

Cover pickles in flour, dredge in egg, then into pork rinds.

AIR FRYER INSTRUCTIONS:

Lay pickles into air fryer basket. Cook for 7 minutes at 400 degrees F.

OVEN INSTRUCTIONS:

Place on a baking sheet. Bake at 425 degrees for 12 minutes or until golden brown.

SAUCE INSTRUCTIONS:

Add vinegar, dill, garlic powder, and sour cream to a mixing bowl. Whisk until combined.

nutrition facts

Amount Per Serving: 1
Servings: 12
Calories 126
Calories from Fat 63
Total Fat 7g (11%)
Saturated Fat 4g (20%)
Cholesterol 42mg (14%)
Sodium 500mg (21%)
Potassium 69mg (2%)
Total Carbohydrate 7g (2%)
Dietary Fiber 3g (12%)
Sugars 1g
Protein 6g (12%)
Vitamin A (4.3%)
Vitamin C (0.6%)
Calcium (4.1%)
Iron (3.5%)

spicy chicken & cheddar empanadas with cilantro sour cream

 30 MINS

 30 MIN

 1 HR

Spicy Chicken Empanadas with Cilantro Sour Cream are perfect to serve during football playoffs. With golden dough and a cheesy, spicy filling they are the ideal game food.

ingredients

DOUGH INGREDIENTS:

- 16 oz mozzarella shredded or cubed
- 4 oz cream cheese
- 1 cup almond flour
- 1/2 cup ground golden flax
- 1/2 cup coconut flour
- 2 tsp baking powder
- 1 tsp salt
- 1 tsp garlic powder
- 2 eggs

SPICY CHICKEN FILLING:

- 2 cups cooked shredded chicken
- 8 oz shredded cheddar cheese
- 4 oz cream cheese softened
- 2-4 tbsp hot sauce
- 1 tsp garlic powder
- 1 tsp ground cumin
- 1/2 tsp dried oregano
- 1/2 tsp salt

CILANTRO SOUR CREAM:

- 16 oz sour cream
- 1 tsp garlic salt
- 1/2 cup chopped fresh cilantro
- 1/2 tsp salt

directions

Preheat oven to 400.

Put mozzarella cheese and cream cheese in a microwave-safe bowl. Microwave one minute. Stir. Microwave 30 seconds. Stir. At this point, all the cheese should be melted. Microwave 30 more seconds until uniform and gloopy (it should look like cheese fondue at this point if it doesn't keep microwaving in 30-second increments). Mix in the eggs and other ingredients. You will need to dump it onto wax paper and knead it by hand to thoroughly incorporate the ingredients or you can do this in a food processor with the dough blade.

Stir together the filling ingredients.

Roll out the dough in between two pieces of parchment paper. Cut 14 four inch circles, rerolling the scraps as necessary until all the dough is used up. I used an upside down plastic container. Divide the filling between the dough circles. Fold the dough over the filling and press the edges together. Optional: use a fork to make little lines around the edge.

Bake for 25-30 minutes until golden brown.

CILANTRO SOUR CREAM:

Stir together all the ingredients. Serve with the empanadas.

nutrition facts

Amount Per Serving: 1

Servings: 14

Calories 417

Calories from Fat 297

Total Fat 33g (51%)

Saturated Fat 16g (80%)

Cholesterol 116mg (39%)

Sodium 922mg (38%)

Potassium 295mg (8%)

Total Carbohydrate 9g (3%)

Dietary Fiber 4g (16%)

Sugars 2g

Protein 21g (42%)

Vitamin A (16.8%)

Vitamin C (2%)

Calcium (40.2%)

Iron (8.3%)

cranberry baked brie

 20 MINS

🔥 25 MIN

🕐 45 MIN

This Baked Brie is covered with sweet cranberry sauce, golden dough, and toasted almonds.

ingredients

DOUGH INGREDIENTS:

- 8 oz mozzarella shredded or cubed
- 2 oz cream cheese
- 1 egg
- 1/3 cup almond flour
- 1/3 cup coconut flour
- 1/3 cup ground golden flax
- 1 tsp baking powder

ASSEMBLY INGREDIENTS:

- 8 oz round brie must be fully enclosed in rind, slices will not work
- 1/4 cup sugar free cranberry sauce
- 1/4 cup sliced almonds
- 1 tbsp sugar-free sweetener

recipe notes

The dough will not cover the whole brie. You will flip it over and no one will ever know. The reason for this is that the dough doesn't cook as well under the cheese. It's easier to just give the impression the brie is completely en-robed in the dough. You could serve this with low carb crackers or fruit, or just eat it with a spoon. When it cools to room temperature you can cut slices and pick them up. But there is something nice about that gooey brie spilling out when you cut into it.

directions

Preheat oven to 400.

Put cheese in a microwave safe bowl. Microwave one minute. Stir. Microwave 30 seconds. Stir. At this point all the cheese should be melted. Microwave 30 more seconds until uniform and gloopy (it should look like cheese fondue at this point). Add the rest of the dough ingredients and the cheese to a food processor. Mix using the dough blade until a uniform color. If you do not have a food processor you can mix in a medium bowl with a wooden spoon but you may need to dump it onto wax paper and knead it by hand to thoroughly incorporate the ingredients.

Press the dough out on a piece of parchment paper into a circle a few inches wider than the brie. Put the cranberry sauce in the middle of the dough. Put the brie on top of the cranberry sauce. Fold the dough up the sides and over a little bit of the brie.

Turn the brie over onto a pie plate or other rimmed baking dish so the cranberry side is up. Sprinkle the nuts on top. Sprinkle the sweetener over the nuts.

Bake for 25 minutes or until the dough is golden.

cranberry sauce recipe:

INGREDIENTS

- 12 oz bag of cranberries
- 4 oz water
- 1 cup sugar-free sweetener
- 1 tsp vanilla
- 1 tsp cinnamon

INSTRUCTIONS:

Combine the cranberries and water in a medium saucepan. Cook over medium heat until all the berries pop, about 5-7 minutes. Add the other ingredients and reduce the heat to low. Cook until desired thickness. It will thicken further as it cools.

Store in the fridge for up to 2 weeks or you can freeze it.

nutrition facts

Amount Per Serving: 1

Servings: 8

Calories 323

Calories from Fat 225

Total Fat 25g (38%)

Saturated Fat 11g (55%)

Cholesterol 79mg (26%)

Sodium 399mg (17%)

Potassium 233mg (7%)

Total Carbohydrate 8g (3%)

Dietary Fiber 4g (16%)

Sugars 1g

Protein 17g (34%)

Vitamin A (9.7%)

Calcium (27.2%)

Iron (7.3%)

chicken stuffed peppers

 10 MINS

 15 MIN

 25 MIN

Chicken stuffed peppers is a quick meal for those busy work days. Sweet mini peppers that are stuffed with chicken, cilantro pesto, spinach, cheese and more baked to a tender and tasty dinner. Mini stuffed peppers are a delicious way to use up peppers from your garden or farmer's market.

ingredients

- 2 cups cooked chicken shredded
- 1/4 cup mayo
- 1/4 cup sour cream
- 1 tbsp cilantro pesto
- 1/2 tsp garlic salt
- 1 cup baby spinach chopped
- 1 cup shredded cheddar
- 12 mini sweet peppers halved and seeded
- sour cream and cilantro optional toppings

directions

Preheat the oven to 400.

Combine the mayo, sour cream, cilantro pesto, and garlic salt. Mix well.

Stir in the chicken, baby spinach, and half the cheddar.

Spoon into mini peppers.

Top with the rest of the cheddar.

Bake for 15-20 minutes until the cheese is golden and bubbly.

Top with sour cream and chopped cilantro.

nutrition facts

Amount Per Serving: 3
Servings: 4
Calories 389
Calories from Fat 225
Total Fat 25g (38%)
Saturated Fat 9g (45%)
Cholesterol 102mg (34%)
Sodium 628mg (26%)
Potassium 508mg (15%)
Total Carbohydrate 7g (2%)
Dietary Fiber 2g (8%)
Sugars 0g
Protein 30g (60%)
Vitamin A (92.8%)
Vitamin C (178.1%)
Calcium (24.5%)
Iron (9%)

chicken cordon bleu stromboli

 20 MINS

25 MIN

45 MIN

If you are looking for a new keto Stromboli Recipe to try you have to try this one. I took the best flavors of my Chicken Cordon Bleu Casserole and made them into a shareable hand-held appetizer perfect for parties and tailgating.

ingredients

DOUGH INGREDIENTS:

- 1 cup mozzarella cheese
- 1 tbsp butter
- 2/3 cup almond flour
- 1 egg
- 1 tsp baking powder

FILLING INGREDIENTS:

- 2 tbsp cream cheese softened
- 1 tbsp butter softened
- 1/2 tsp garlic powder
- 1/2 tsp mustard
- 1/2 cup shredded chicken
- 1/2 cup shredded baby swiss
- 1/2 cup ham

directions

Preheat oven to 400.

Put mozzarella cheese in a microwave-safe bowl. Microwave one minute. Stir. Microwave 30 seconds. Stir. At this point, all the cheese should be melted. Microwave 30 more seconds until uniform and gloopy (it should look like cheese fondue at this point). Mix in the butter until it melts and then add the egg, flours, and baking powder. You will need to dump it onto wax paper and knead it by hand to thoroughly incorporate the ingredients or you can do this in a food processor with the dough blade.

Press or roll into a large rectangle on a parchment lined baking sheet using wet hands. Mix together the cream cheese, butter, garlic powder, and mustard in a medium bowl until well combined. Stir in the chicken, ham, and cheese. Place spoonfuls down the center of the rectangle. Roll into a log.

Bake for 25-30 minutes or until golden brown.

nutrition facts

Amount Per Serving: 1

Servings: 8

Calories 281

Calories from Fat 207

Total Fat 23g (35%)

Saturated Fat 7g (35%)

Cholesterol 67mg (22%)

Sodium 362mg (15%)

Potassium 143mg (4%)

Total Carbohydrate 5g (2%)

Dietary Fiber 2g (8%)

Sugars 1g

Protein 15g (30%)

Vitamin A (7.3%)

Vitamin C (0%)

Calcium (22.4%)

Iron (6.3%)

Chapter Two

cold appetizers & dips

blt dip

10 MINS

10 MINS

My fabulous BLT Dip has the flavors of a BLT sandwich in dip form. It can be served warm or cold and is perfect for a summer bbq or party. Or any other time of the year.

ingredients

- 1 lb bacon (cooked until crisp and chopped or 5 oz of bacon crumbles)
- 8 oz cream cheese
- 1/4 cup mayo
- 1/4 cup sour cream
- 1/4 cup shredded cheddar
- 1 tsp onion powder
- 1 tsp dried minced garlic
- 1/2 tsp smoked paprika (or regular, but the smoked compliments the bacon nicely)
- pinch of salt
- 1 cup chopped lettuce
- 1 cup chopped tomato (squeeze out the juice after chopping)
- fresh veggies to dip

directions

Combine 1/3 of the bacon with the cream cheese, sour cream, mayo, cheddar, and seasonings.

Mix in a deep dish pie plate. Sprinkle on the lettuce, tomato, and the rest of the bacon.

Serve with fresh veggies to dip.

nutrition facts

Amount Per Serving: 1

Servings: 12

Calories278

Calories from Fat 234

Total Fat 26g (40%)

Saturated Fat 10g (60%)

Cholesterol 52mg (17%)

Sodium 388mg (16%)

Potassium 156mg (4%)

Total Carbohydrate 2g (1%)

Dietary Fiber 0g (0%)

Protein 6g (12%)

Vitamin A (8.3%)

Vitamin C (2.5%)

Calcium (5%)

Iron (2.7%)

roasted red pepper dip

 5 MINS

5 MINS

This Roasted Red Pepper Dip will quickly become your go-to accompaniment to chips and raw veggies. It is full of flavor with roasted peppers and garlic.

ingredients

- 10 cloves of garlic
- 12 oz jar roasted red peppers drained
- 2/3 cup mayo
- 5.3 oz coconut cream
- 1 tbsp tomato paste
- 1 tsp xanthan gum
- 1/2 tsp salt

directions

Finely chop the garlic in a food processor, scraping down the sides if needed.

Add the rest of the ingredients and pulse until the roasted red peppers are chopped.

Serve with raw vegetables or low carb chips.

nutrition facts

Amount Per Serving: 1

Servings: 12

Calories: 137

Calories from Fat 117

Total Fat 13g (20%)

Saturated Fat 5g (25%)

Cholesterol 5mg (2%)

Sodium 570mg (24%)

Potassium 105mg (3%)

Total Carbohydrate 3g (1%)

Dietary Fiber 1g (4%)

Protein 1g (2%)

Vitamin A (3.5%)

Vitamin C (17.7%)

Calcium (1.9%)

Iron (3.4%)

bacon cheddar mini cheese balls

 5 MINS

5 MINS

If you need a quick and easy appetizer stop right here. My Bacon Cheddar Mini Cheese Balls have only 3 ingredients but a ton of flavor. They come together in just 5 minutes.

ingredients

- 8 oz shredded cheddar cheese
- 8 oz cream cheese softened
- 2 cups bacon crumbles

directions

Microwave the bacon crumbles for about thirty seconds. This crisps them up so they taste fresh. (If you do not have a microwave you can just skip this step or pan fry them for a minute or two).

Stir together the cream cheese and shredded cheddar. Use a small cookie scoop to scoop tablespoon sized balls. Roll them in the bacon crumbles. Serve immediately or refrigerate for later.

This makes about 30 mini cheese balls.

nutrition facts

Amount Per Serving:3

Servings: 30

Calories 192

Calories from Fat 153

Total Fat 17g (26%)

Saturated Fat 9g (45%)

Cholesterol 52mg (17%)

Sodium 250mg (10%)

Potassium 64mg (2%)

Total Carbohydrate 1g (0%)

Dietary Fiber 0g (0%)

Protein 7g (14%)

Vitamin A (10.6%)

Calcium (18.6%)

Iron (1.5%)

mediterranean cheese spread

 5 MINS

5 MINS

Loaded with olives, basil, sun-dried tomatoes, and artichokes this Mediterranean cheese spread recipe is the perfect easy flavorful appetizer. A whirl in the food processor and its ready to serve. Enjoy hot or cold with veggies low carb crackers chips or pita bread.

ingredients

- 16 oz cream cheese
- 1 cup black olives
- 1 cup kalamata olives
- 1 cup marinated artichoke hearts
- 1/2 cup sun-dried tomatoes softened
- 2 tbsp fresh basil packed
- low carb pita bread optional

directions

Pulse the cream cheese in the food processor until smooth.

Add the olives, artichokes, and sun-dried tomatoes.

Pulse until coarsely chopped.

Add the basil.

Pulse until mixed into the cheese spread.

recipe notes

1) To soften the sun-dried tomatoes simply cover them in hot water for five minutes. Drain the water and use as directed.

2) You can make this cheese spread as smooth or chunky as you like. Pulse gently until it is your desired texture. I like it with small pieces of the chopped vegetables in it.

3) To make low carb pita bread simply bake the dough for the stromboli found on page 26 in two small circles. Cut into wedges, drizzle with olive oil, and sprinkle with salt.

nutrition facts

Amount Per Serving: 1
Servings: 16
Calories 144
Calories from Fat 117
Total Fat 13g (20%)
Saturated Fat 5g (25%)
Cholesterol 31mg (10%)
Sodium 409mg (17%)
Potassium 164mg (5%)
Total Carbohydrate 4g (1%)
Dietary Fiber 1g (4%)
Protein 2g (4%)
Vitamin A (12.4%)
Vitamin C (4.9%)
Calcium (4.3%)
Iron (3.3%)

creamy chive dip

 5 MINS

 5 MINS

The best dips are quick, easy, and full of flavor. This Creamy Chive Dip doesn't disappoint. It has only 5 ingredients and 5 minutes to prep but is irresistible.

ingredients

- 1 cup plain greek yogurt
- 1 cup mayo
- 1/2 cup unsweetened almond milk
- handful of chives 1 cup loosely packed
- 1 tsp salt

directions

Combine all the ingredients in a food processor and process until smooth.

Alternatively, combine the almond milk and chives in a rocket blender and blend until the chives are finely chopped. Whisk in a medium bowl with the rest of the ingredients until smooth.

nutrition facts

Amount Per Serving: 1

Servings: 10

Calories 166

Calories from Fat 153

Total Fat 17g (26%)

Saturated Fat 2g (10%)

Cholesterol 10mg (3%)

Sodium 398mg (17%)

Potassium 38mg (1%)

Total Carbohydrate 0g (0%)

Dietary Fiber 0g (0%)

Protein 2g (4%)

Vitamin A (2%)

Vitamin C (1.4%)

Calcium (4.1%)

Iron (0.4%)

feta & dill cheese ball

 5 MINS

5 MINS

The best dips are quick, easy, and full of flavor. This Creamy Chive Dip doesn't disappoint. It has only 5 ingredients and 5 minutes to prep but is irresistible.

ingredients

- 16 oz low-fat cream cheese softened ***
- 8 oz crumbled feta
- 8 oz shredded mozzarella
- 2 tbsp fresh dill chopped
- 2 tbsp fresh dill optional, to coat the cheese ball

directions

Mix together the first four ingredients. Form into two balls and roll in plastic wrap. Store in the fridge until ready to serve. Serve with crackers or fresh veggies.

Optional: Before serving roll in extra chopped dill or chopped nuts.

recipe notes

I prefer the tang of neufchatal (low fat) cream cheese to complement the feta in this recipe but you can use full-fat cream cheese if you prefer.

nutrition facts

Amount Per Serving: 1

Servings: 12

Calories: 96

Calories from Fat: 63

Total Fat 7g (11%)

Saturated Fat 4g (22%)

Cholesterol 26mg (9%)

Sodium 213mg (9%)

Potassium 0mg (0%)

Total Carbohydrate 2g (1%)

Dietary Fiber 0g (0%)

Sugars: 2g

Protein 5g (10%)

Vitamin A (3%)

Vitamin C (0%)

Calcium (8%)

Iron (1%)

Chapter Three

hot dips to share

jalapeno popper dip

10 MINS

30 MINS

40 MINS

Jalapeno Popper Dip is perfect for entertaining or when you just want finger food for dinner. It is creamy, cheesy, loaded with bacon, and has as much of a kick as you want.

ingredients

DIP INGREDIENTS:

- 8 oz cream cheese softened
- 1/2 cup mayo
- 1/2 cup sour cream
- 1/4 - 1 cup jalapeno seeded and diced ***
- 1/2 cup bacon crumbles
- 4 oz cheddar
- 1/4 tsp salt
- 3 cups chopped cooked chicken or steamed cauliflower

TOPPING INGREDIENTS:

- 1 jalapeno thinly sliced and seeded
- 4 oz cheddar
- 1/2 cup bacon crumbles

directions

Preheat the oven to 350.

Combine the dip ingredients and spread in a pie plate.

Top with the remaining topping ingredients.

Bake for 30-40 minutes until hot and bubbly.

recipe notes

I'm a bit of a wimp when it comes to spicy food. I used 1/4 cup chopped jalapeno and it had a slight kick. I think I'm going to brave 1/2 cup next time. If you enjoy spicy food you can use a full cup and keep the seeds in.

nutrition facts

Amount Per Serving: 1

Servings: 8

Calories 440

Calories from Fat 360

Total Fat 40g (62%)

Saturated Fat 17g (85%)

Cholesterol 108mg (36%)

Sodium 493mg (21%)

Potassium 167mg (5%)

Total Carbohydrate 2g (1%)

Dietary Fiber 0g (0%)

Protein 17g (34%)

Vitamin A (16.8%)

Vitamin C (3.5%)

Calcium (25.3%)

Iron (4.1%)

sausage dip with cream cheese

 10 MINS

 20 MINS

30 MINS

This Sausage Dip with Cream Cheese is a fantastic make-ahead party appetizer. Prep it a day or two before, bake and serve with veggies or low carb pita dippers. It is packed with flavor and has only 5 ingredients!

ingredients

- 1 lb sausage
- 1 cup frozen spinach thawed
- 1/4 cup sundried tomatoes chopped
- 8 oz cream cheese
- 1 tsp salt
- 1 cup shredded mozzarella

directions

Preheat oven to 400 (if serving immediately).

Brown the sausage in a large skillet.

Add the spinach, sundried tomatoes, cream cheese, and salt. Stir until the cream cheese melts and is thoroughly incorporated.

Spread in a pie plate or small casserole dish. Top with the mozzarella cheese. Refrigerate if making ahead.

If serving immediately bake for 20 minutes.

If preparing ahead of time bake at 400 for 30 minutes until the cheese is melted and golden and the dip is hot in the middle.

recipe notes

See page 36 for instructions to make low carb pita dippers.

nutrition facts

Amount Per Serving: 1

Servings: 16

Calories 1162

Calories from Fat 126

Total Fat 14g (22%)

Saturated Fat 6g (30%)

Cholesterol 41mg (14%)

Sodium 426mg (18%)

Potassium 187mg (5%)

Total Carbohydrate 2g (1%)

Dietary Fiber 0g (0%)

Protein 7g (14%)

Vitamin A (28.3%)

Vitamin C (1.7%)

Calcium (6.6%)

Iron (4.1%)

layered taco dip with meat

5 MINS

25 MINS

30 MINS

Taco Dip. At any party or gathering, I've been to it is always one of the first appetizers to disappear. We love this Easy Layered Taco Dip with Meat so much that I even make it for dinner sometimes.

ingredients

- 8 oz cream cheese
- 1 lb ground turkey or other ground meat browned and drained
- 1 tbsp taco seasoning
- 1 cup salsa
- 1 cup shredded cheddar

directions

Preheat oven to 350.

Spread the softened cream cheese in the bottom of a deep dish pie plate.

Mix together the cooked meat and taco seasoning. Spread on top of the cream cheese.

Spoon the salsa on top and spread.

Sprinkle the cheese on. Bake for 25-30 minutes or until hot and golden.

nutrition facts

Amount Per Serving: 1
Servings: 10
Calories 181
Calories from Fat 108
Total Fat 12g (18%)
Saturated Fat 6g (30%)
Cholesterol 61mg (20%)
Sodium 370mg (15%)
Potassium 250mg (7%)
Total Carbohydrate 2g (1%)
Dietary Fiber 0g (0%)
Protein 15g (30%)
Vitamin A (11.6%)
Vitamin C (0.7%)
Calcium (11.3%)
Iron (3.4%)

easy sausage pizza dip

 5 MINS

 15 MINS

 20 MINS

This Sausage Pizza Dip will be your favorite party dip. It has all the flavors of the best sausage pizza in an easy and healthy dip that pairs perfectly with fresh veggies.

ingredients

- 8 oz cream cheese softened
- 1/2 cup no sugar added pasta sauce
- 2 cups cooked crumbled sausage about 1 pound
- 1 cup shredded mozzarella
- 1/4 cup parmesan cheese

directions

Preheat the oven to 400.

Spread the cream cheese in the bottom of a deep dish pie plate. Spread the tomato sauce on top. Top with the cooked sausage. Sprinkle with the mozzarella and parmesan.

Bake for 15 minutes until bubbly and golden brown around the edges.

recipe notes

If you need to cook sausage for this recipe do
that first. I like to cook and crumble a big batch
and freeze it in 1 cup portions for recipes. I cut
the casings off with scissors (so much easier
than trying to squish out the meat), put them in
a big frying pan coated with cooking spray, and
just cook until brown. I break up the pieces with
a potato masher a few times while it cooks.

nutrition facts

Amount Per Serving: 1
Servings: 8
Calories 334
Calories from Fat 261
Total Fat 29g (45%)
Saturated Fat 13g (65%)
Cholesterol 86mg (29%)
Sodium 685mg (29%)
Potassium 274mg (7%)
Total Carbohydrate 2g (1%)
Dietary Fiber 0g (0%)
Sugars 1g
Protein 15g (30%)
Vitamin A (12.2%)
Vitamin C (1.8%)
Calcium (14.3%)
Iron (5.6%)

bacon spinach dip

15 MINS

25 MINS

40 MINS

This is the ultimate spinach dip recipe! I've eaten spinach dip so very many times in my life but this one beats them all. It is cheesy, creamy, garlicky, and perfect with fresh veggies or crackers.

ingredients

- 12 oz. bacon cooked until crisp and crumbled
- 4 oz cream cheese
- 1/4 cup mayo
- 1/4 cup sour cream
- 1 tsp garlic powder
- 1/2 cup grated parmesan cheese
- 16 oz frozen spinach thawed and drained well
- 6 oz shredded mozzarella

directions

Preheat oven to 350.

Cook bacon until crisp, drain, and crumbled or chop it into small pieces.

In a large bowl mix the cream cheese, mayo, garlic powder, and parmesan cheese. Mix in the spinach, half the bacon, and half the mozzarella.

Spread in a deep dish pie plate. Sprinkle the remaining mozzarella and bacon on top.

Bake at 350 until hot and bubbly. About 15 minutes.

recipe notes

Alternatively, you can microwave the dip for about 5 minutes. The only down side to microwaving is the cheese doesn't get golden on top. But on a hot summer day that is a sacrifice I am willing to make.

Also, if you are an artichoke fan feel free to add some for a Bacon Caesar Spinach Artichoke Dip.

nutrition facts

Amount Per Serving: 1

Servings: 8

Calories 396

Calories from Fat 315

Total Fat 35g (54%)

Saturated Fat 13g (65%)

Cholesterol 72mg (24%)

Sodium 648mg (27%)

Potassium 338mg (10%)

Total Carbohydrate 4g (1%)

Dietary Fiber 1g (4%)

Sugars 1g

Protein 15g (30%)

Vitamin A (141.9%)

Vitamin C (3.8%)

Calcium (27.4%)

Iron (8.1%)

Chapter Five

snacks & finger foods

turkey bacon ranch pinwheels

 5 MINS

5 MINS

Turkey Bacon Ranch Pinwheels are a crowd-pleasing, five-minute prep appetizer. My kids gobbled these up when I made them for the Super Bowl. They have a lot of flavor with only a little bit of effort.

ingredients

- 6 oz cream cheese
- 12 slices smoked deli turkey, about 3 oz
- 1/4 tsp each garlic powder dill, and minced onion
- 1 tbsp bacon crumbles
- 2 tbsp finely shredded cheddar cheese

directions

Put the cream cheese between 2 pieces of plastic wrap. Roll it out until it's about 1/4 inch thick. Peel off the top piece of plastic wrap. Lay the slices of turkey on top of the cream cheese.

Cover with a new piece of plastic wrap and flip the whole thing over. Peel off the piece of plastic that is now on the top. Sprinkle the spices on top of the cream cheese. Sprinkle with the bacon and cheese.

Roll up the pinwheels so that the turkey is on the outside. Refrigerate for at least 2 hours. Thinly slice and serve on top of low carb crackers or sliced cucumber.

nutrition facts

Amount Per Serving: 1

Servings: 6

Calories: 141

Calories from Fat 108

Total Fat 12g (18%)

Saturated Fat 6g (30%)

Cholesterol 43mg (14%)

Sodium 328mg (14%)

Potassium 71mg (2%)

Total Carbohydrate 2g (1%)

Dietary Fiber 0g (0%)

Sugars 1g

Protein 5g (10%)

Vitamin A (8.6%)

Calcium (6.5%)

Iron (1.8%)

glazed cinnamon vanilla almonds

 5 MINS

 5 MINS

 10 MINS

These Glazed Cinnamon Vanilla Almonds are the perfect sweet treat for when you are on the go. You can keep a little container in your purse to help avoid tempting sweets on the road.

ingredients

- 2.5 cups roasted salted almonds
- 1/2 cup sugar-free sweetener
- 1 tsp vanilla
- 1 tsp cinnamon

directions

In a medium saucepan over medium heat cook the sweetener until it is melted. Add the vanilla and cinnamon. Remove from heat.

Add the almonds. Stir every 10-15 minutes as they cool. The syrup will continue to thicken and harden.

Once they are coated with all the syrup pour onto a piece of parchment or waxed paper. Cool completely, still stirring occasionally. Store in an air tight container.

recipe notes

Notes on Sweeteners: I use my own blend of xylitol, erythritol, and stevia in my recipes. This is twice as sweet as sugar. It is comparable to Trim Healthy Mama Gentle Sweet and Truvia.

To sub in Swerve use 1.5 to 2 times the amount of sweetener called for.

To sub in Pyure or Trim Healthy Mama Super Sweet use half the amount of sweetener called for.

Substitutions will work in most recipes. They may not work in candies, such as caramel.

nutrition facts

Servings: 12
Calories 172
Calories from Fat 126
Total Fat 12g (22%)
Saturated Fat 1g (5%)
Sodium 0mg (0%)
Potassium 210mg (6%)
Total Carbohydrate 6g (2%)
Dietary Fiber 3g (12%)
Sugars 1g
Protein 6g (12%)
Calcium (8.1%)
Iron (6.3%)

low carb cheddar garlic cheese crisps

 10 MINS

 15 MINS

 25 MINS

Need a salty snack? Try my cheddar garlic cheese crisps! They are low carb, keto, and gluten-free!

ingredients

- 7 tbsp butter softened
- 3 oz cream cheese softened
- 1/3 cup coconut flour
- 1/3 cup almond flour
- 1/3 cup golden flax meal
- 1/2 tsp dried minced garlic
- 1/4 tsp salt
- 1/2 cup shredded cheddar

directions

Preheat oven to 350. Line a baking sheet with parchment paper.

Mix all ingredients with a wooden spoon in a medium bowl. It should come together easily if the butter and cream were at room temperature. I kneaded it with my hands for a few minutes to make sure it was mixed thoroughly.

To make cheese crisps/straws: Put the dough in a cookie press with the bumpy line attachment. (Descriptive, I know. Basically it's a one inch line opening with one flat side and one side with ridges). Press the dough through the cookie press onto a parchment lined baking sheet. If desired brush with extra melted butter and sprinkle with a tiny bit of garlic powder. Bake for 12-15 min out until golden brown.

To make crackers: Roll out the dough between two pieces of parchment paper until it is about 1/4 inch thick. Remove the top piece. Cut with a pizza cutter into squares. If desired brush with extra melted butter and sprinkle with a tiny bit of garlic powder. Bake for 15-20 min out until golden brown.

nutrition facts

Amount Per Serving: 1

Servings: 8

Calories 237

Calories from Fat 189

Total Fat 21g (32%)

Saturated Fat 11g (55%)

Cholesterol 45mg (15%)

Sodium 252mg (11%)

Potassium 75mg (2%)

Total Carbohydrate 6g (2%)

Dietary Fiber 4g (16%)

Sugars 1g

Protein 5g (10%)

Vitamin A (10.5%)

Calcium (9.1%)

Iron (4.3%)

3 ingredient stovetop glazed pecans

 2 MINS

 8 MINS

 10 MINS

This sweet glazed pecans only require a few minutes and three ingredients!

ingredients

- 1 tbsp butter
- 1/4 cup sugar-free sweetener
- 1 cup pecan halves

directions

Add the butter and sweetener to a medium saucepan. Heat on medium until melted. Add the pecans and cook for about 5-8 minutes until the syrup begins turning brown and the pecans smell toasted. Remove from the heat. Stir every 5 minutes as they cool. The syrup will continue to thicken. Once they are well coated and room temperature transfer to a waxed paper lined baking sheet. Refrigerate until the coating is hard.

recipe notes

Notes on Sweeteners: I use my own blend of xylitol, erythritol, and stevia in my recipes. This is twice as sweet as sugar. It is comparable to Trim Healthy Mama Gentle Sweet and Truvia.

To sub in Swerve use 1.5 to 2 times the amount of sweetener called for.

To sub in Pyure or Trim Healthy Mama Super Sweet use half the amount of sweetener called for.

Substitutions will work in most recipes. They may not work in candies, such as caramel.

nutrition facts

Amount Per Serving: 1
Servings: 4
Calories 196
Calories from Fat 180
Total Fat 20g (31%)
Saturated Fat 3g (15%)
Cholesterol 7mg (2%)
Sodium 25mg (1%)
Potassium 101mg (3%)
Total Carbohydrate 3g (1%)
Dietary Fiber 2g (8%)
Sugars 0g
Protein 2g (4%)
Vitamin A (2.1%)
Vitamin C (0.3%)
Calcium (1.7%)
Iron (3.5%)

Made in the USA
Monee, IL
14 November 2020